PRETEEN PRESSURES

ALCOHOL

by Paula McGuire

RSVP

RAINTREE STECK-VAUGHN
PUBLISHERS
The Steck-Vaughn Company

Austin, Texas

Consultants

Joann Baumgarten, Social Worker, Family Service Association of Bucks County, PA
William B. Presnell, Clinical Member, American Association for Marriage and Family Therapy

Developed for Steck-Vaughn Company by
Visual Education Corporation, Princeton, New Jersey
Project Director: Jewel Moulthrop
Editorial Assistant: Jacqueline Morais
Photo Research: Sara Matthews
Electronic Preparation: Cynthia C. Feldner, Manager; Fiona Torphy
Production Supervisor: Ellen Foos
Electronic Production: Lisa Evans-Skopas, Manager; Elise Dodeles, Deirdre Sheean, Isabelle Verret
Interior Design: Maxson Crandall

Raintree Steck-Vaughn Publishers staff
Editor: Kathy DeVico
Project Manager: Joyce Spicer

Photo Credits: Cover: © David Young-Wolff/PhotoEdit; 6: © Aneal Vohra/Unicorn Stock Photos; 9: © Tony Freeman/PhotoEdit; 15: © Bill Bachmann/PhotoEdit; 16: © David Young-Wolff/PhotoEdit; 19: © David Young-Wolff/PhotoEdit; 23: © David R. Frazier/ Photo Researchers, Inc.; 26: © Tom Prettyman/PhotoEdit; 27: © Dennis MacDonald/ PhotoEdit; 34: © Dana White/PhotoEdit; 37: © Bill Aron/PhotoEdit; 38: © Michelle Bridwell/PhotoEdit; 42: © Aneal Vohra/Unicorn Stock Photos

Library of Congress Cataloging-in-Publication Data
McGuire, Paula.
    Alcohol/by Paula McGuire.
       p.   cm. — (Preteen pressures)
    Includes bibliographical references and index.
    Summary: Discusses how alcohol affects the body, dangers and consequences of drinking too much, and how to handle peer pressure and living with an alcoholic parent.
    ISBN 0-8172-5026-3
    1. Alcoholism—United States—Prevention—Juvenile literature. 2. Alcoholism—Treatment—United States—Juvenile literature. 3. Youth—Alcohol use—United States—Juvenile literature. 4. Children of alcoholics—United States—Juvenile literature. [1. Alcoholism.] I. Title. II. Series.
HV5066.M37 1998
362.29'2'0973—dc21
                                97-22371
                                  CIP

Printed and bound in the United States
1 2 3 4 5 6 7 8 9 0 LB 01 00 99 98 97

CONTENTS

INTRODUCTION

Alcohol is the most widely accepted and abused drug in the United States today. It affects the lives of millions of people—at their jobs and in their homes. It causes thousands of deaths every year, especially on the roads. It costs millions of dollars in medical care.

Alcohol use often starts at a young age. Many 8th graders have tried drinking. Many 12th graders drink regularly. More than half of the nation's junior and senior high school students drink beer or other alcoholic beverages. Many parents drink and do not tell their children not to. TV shows and movies suggest that drinking is part of the good life, and children buy that message. The law in every state except one says that you can't drink under the age of 21. But nobody pays much attention. Alcohol is easy for kids to get.

Experts can predict who is likely to become a problem drinker. Even if you don't drink now, here are some questions for you to answer:

- ▶ Does anyone in your family often drink alcohol or use other drugs?

- ▶ Do any of the adults in your family drink to avoid facing their problems?

- ▶ Do you often feel unloved by your family?

- ▶ Do you often feel that you don't "fit in"?

- ▶ Do you have problems in school?

- ▶ Do you break rules or participate in activities that make parents, teachers, and other adults unhappy?

- ▶ Are you spending more and more time alone?

The more yes answers you gave to these questions, the more likely you are to become a problem drinker. If you already have a problem with alcohol, talk about it now with somebody you trust. If you have never drunk alcohol but are feeling pressured by friends to drink, <u>DON'T!</u> Think about your future now. Don't wait until it's too late.

The sooner you learn about alcohol, the better you can choose whether or not to drink. This book will provide you with lots of information about alcohol and drinking. Learning about alcohol will help you make a healthy choice. If you have questions, ask your parents or another adult. It's up to you to keep your future healthy, happy, and safe.

When underage drinking is involved, a pleasant event may become an unpleasant and painful experience.

HOW ALCOHOL AFFECTS THE BODY

" My name is Elena. A few weeks ago, my sister Isabel gave a party. My parents were away that weekend. They left Isabel in charge of me and of the house. Isabel told me that she was having some of her high school friends over on Saturday night. She told me that I could hang around for a while, if I wouldn't tell our parents about the party.

I was pretty excited about being at the party. Everybody was downstairs in the den, and there was music and dancing. One of the boys asked me to dance. He was really nice. When we finished dancing, he asked me if I'd like something to drink. I was hot and thirsty and drank the bottle of juice he gave me.

I danced with other people. It was warm in the room, and I drank some more juice. Then it got really hot. I began to feel dizzy. Things started to look strange and move crazily around in the room. I know I wanted to go outside for some air. All I remember is throwing up in the kitchen sink. **"**

Elena has just described the first time she drank alcohol. The "juice" she thought she had been drinking was actually a wine cooler. Nobody told her what she was drinking. The wine was disguised by the sweet taste of the fruit juices that were mixed with it. She became drunk and then ill. What had started out as a wonderful evening turned into an embarrassing and unpleasant experience for her. All too often, this is the way preteens and teens are introduced to alcohol. They take the first drink without understanding what alcohol does to the body.

WHAT IS ALCOHOL?

The alcohol in an alcoholic beverage is called ethyl alcohol. An alcoholic beverage is made by fermentation. Fermentation is the process of changing grains or fruit into ethyl alcohol. There are three main kinds of alcoholic beverages. Beer is made from grains. Wine is made from grapes or other fruit. Distilled spirits—which include brandy, gin, rum, vodka, and whiskey—are usually made from grains. But they are also made from other plants. Vodka is made from potatoes; rum is made from molasses, which comes from sugar and sweet vegetables. Distilled spirits are made by boiling and condensing alcohol into a stronger and purer form. Flavoring and color are often added. Distilled spirits are sometimes called liquor or hard liquor.

The percentage of alcohol varies in different beverages.

Beer:	2–8	percent
Wine cooler:	4–7	percent
Wine:	8–20	percent
Distilled spirits:	40–50	percent

Alcohol has been manufactured and consumed by people around the world for thousands of years. It has been used as food, as medicine, or as part of religious ceremonies. Alcohol is also a part of many social occasions, such as weddings, funerals, and smaller gatherings among friends. Alcohol has played a large part in American social life since colonial days.

Drunkenness (or intoxication) is always the result of having drunk too much alcohol. Such behavior has been criticized throughout history. Excessive drinking was the concern of American reformers who led a drive to ban the use of alcohol in the late 1800s and early 1900s.

Today alcoholic beverages are usually served by the bottle, the can, or the glass. Although they are different sizes, each of these alcoholic beverages contains the same amount of alcohol—about half an ounce.

HOW ALCOHOL IS ABSORBED BY THE BODY

Alcohol moves through the body quickly. It takes only a few minutes to race through the stomach, the heart, and the bloodstream to reach the brain. Alcohol is a poison to the body, so the body tries to remove it quickly by increasing blood flow and blood pressure. About 10 percent of the alcohol that a person drinks is removed from the body in urine or sweat. The liver must process, or break down, the rest (90 percent) of the alcohol into water and carbon dioxide. The liver can process only about half an ounce of alcohol in about one and a half hours.

THE EFFECTS OF DRINKING ALCOHOL

Alcohol affects each person in a different way, depending on the person's age, sex, weight, and mood. Smaller and younger people—usually women, children, and teens—are affected faster than men and larger people. People who drink alcohol regularly will have built up a tolerance for it. People who drink less will be more strongly affected by the same amount of alcohol.

Alcohol is a depressant drug. This means that it affects the brain and nerve cells by slowing them down. Even a small amount of alcohol may:

▶ Cause sleepiness

▶ Cause lack of attention and loss of memory

▶ Affect vision and sensitivity to pain, taste, and smell

- ▶ Trigger allergies
- ▶ Interact dangerously with medications, such as aspirin

Alcohol also causes changes in behavior. People may become depressed, laugh wildly, or be very rude. Even a small amount of alcohol can cause drunkenness. Drunkenness in its extreme form may include vomiting or loss of consciousness. If a drinker binge drinks (drinks more than five drinks in less than an hour), he or she may become very ill from alcohol poisoning. Many young people die this way each year.

Time alone will allow a drunk person to become sober. Coffee, tea, cold air, a cold shower, or exercise will not work. The body must have the time to process the alcohol—about three hours for one ounce. Likewise, there is no cure but time for a hangover that follows the next day. Hangovers include headache, nausea, shakiness, weakness, and sensitivity to sound and light. Thirst is a common symptom of a hangover because alcohol causes the body to lose water.

LONG-TERM EFFECTS OF HEAVY DRINKING

Heavy drinking causes harm to all body organs, especially the brain, heart, and liver. People who abuse alcohol can permanently damage brain and nerve cells. They may have blackouts (temporary loss of vision, consciousness, or memory) and hallucinations (seeing or hearing things that are not really there). Heavy drinking may cause a person's heart to become enlarged or to beat irregularly. Alcohol raises the blood pressure and heart rate, increasing the risk of stroke or heart attack. Alcohol abuse damages the liver, causing alcoholic hepatitis (liver inflammation) and cirrhosis (a permanent disease that kills liver cells and leads to liver failure).

Alcohol harms the immune system and opens the way for serious infections. Long-term drinkers also have an increased risk for cancer and HIV (the virus that causes AIDS). People who drink sometimes forget about the importance of using condoms for safer sex.

People who abuse alcohol may become malnourished. Although alcohol is high in calories and sugar, it provides no nutrients for the body. It also interferes with the body's ability to absorb vitamins C and A, calcium, and certain minerals.

CAUSES OF ALCOHOLISM

The U.S. Department of Health and Human Services classifies alcohol as a drug. Yet people drink alcohol. It is the most used and abused drug in the United States.

Alcohol is easy to find—in liquor stores, grocery stores, restaurants, ballparks, theaters and concert halls, at picnics, and in private homes. People drink alcohol with meals and at parties. The average American adult drinks more than 2 gallons of liquor, more than 2 gallons of wine, and more than 30 gallons of beer in a year.

ALCOHOL AND ADVERTISING

Alcohol is big business in the United States. In 1990 companies in this country produced 8 billion gallons of alcoholic beverages, about 75 percent of which was beer. The alcohol industry employs researchers to find new markets for their products. Alcohol manufacturers also advertise heavily. Alcoholic beverages are advertised in magazines and newspapers; on television, radio, and outdoor billboards; on trains, subways, buses, and airplanes—in fact, anywhere that advertising appears.

Alcohol is also linked to sports in the United States. Alcohol companies often hire popular sports figures to appear in their ads. Beer commercials are common during televised sports events. Athletic events are often sponsored by beer companies, and arenas and stadiums are decorated with large and colorful advertisements for alcoholic beverages.

Alcohol companies claim that their ads are intended for people who already drink, especially men and sports fans. Some people disagree with this statement, however. They argue that advertisements for alcoholic beverages are often aimed at underage people and at women. How often have you seen images on your TV screen of young men and women drinking beer and having a good time? They appear in a warm and friendly group at home, in a bar, at the beach, or on the ski slopes. These images lead you to believe that such people are happy and popular. They suggest that if you drink a certain beer, too, you can be just like those people in the ad.

Advertisements for alcoholic beverages—often appearing in college newspapers and other publications for young people—rarely remind you that alcohol is illegal for those under 21. Neither do they warn their readers about the dangers of drinking. People under 21 spend many hours a week watching television. They are bound to be influenced by the number of alcohol advertisements they see. It is not surprising that the alcohol industry spends more than $1 billion a year for advertising. This is one reason why alcohol is such a widely accepted part of American life.

In the past, people who were alcoholics were thought to be weak or bad. Only during the last few decades have scientists begun to question whether alcoholism might have something to do with genetics. Genetics is the branch of biology that deals with heredity—the genes or characteristics you inherit from your family. Researchers know that some diseases are passed on from parents to children through genes. They wonder if alcoholism is passed on in the same way.

For one thing, alcoholism tends to run in families. Children of alcoholics will not always become alcoholics. But they are more likely to be alcoholics than children from families in which there are no alcoholics. Researchers believe that there are two reasons for this: genetics and family environment.

Social environment affects a person's views about alcohol. By observing their parents and other adults having a good time without alcohol, these children are learning that alcohol is not a necessary part of a social event.

Alcoholism

Alcoholism is a serious illness. Alcoholism is chronic—it continues for a long time. And it is progressive—it becomes worse. Alcoholism interferes with a drinker's personal and professional life. Without treatment the alcoholic is unable to stop drinking.

Alcoholism is a serious illness that can eventually lead to death.

And the only way for an alcoholic to recover is to stop drinking. Otherwise, he or she may die.

Some people drink too much because they have family problems or work-related problems. They use alcohol as an escape from their problems. The drinker may show signs of poor health or a change in personality or behavior. Once the problems are solved, however, the drinker often stops drinking. Sometimes he or she drinks on social occasions, such as a wedding or a special dinner.

Other drinkers become dependent on alcohol and cannot stop drinking. They crave alcohol. Soon they need more drinks to get the same effect that they used to get from a few drinks. This is alcoholism, and it is widespread in the United States:

▶ Alcoholism is a leading cause of early death in the United States after cancer and heart disease.

▶ About 15 million American adults experience problems at home and at work that are related to drinking alcohol.
Source: *Seventh Special Report to the U.S. Congress on Alcohol and Health*, U.S. Department of Health and Human Services, 1990.

▶ About 76 million adult Americans have been exposed to alcoholism in their families during their lives.
Source: Survey conducted by the National Council for Health Statistics and the National Clearinghouse for Alcohol and Drug Information, 1991.

▶ "Of all the substances Americans are likely to abuse or become addicted to, alcohol is far and away the leader—particularly among teenagers."
Source: "A Sobering Reality," *Scholastic Update*, November 16, 1990.

EFFECTS OF ALCOHOL ABUSE

The effects of alcohol abuse go far beyond the drinkers themselves. As the drinker's health worsens, so does his or her ability to lead a normal, useful life. Alcoholics may become violent, depressed, and suicidal. They may take their own lives. They may cause accidents that kill other people. Their behavior can break up families and cause losses of time and money in the workplace. As a result, alcoholism is a problem for society as a whole.

IN FAMILIES

The families of alcoholics often suffer greatly. They often try to keep up the appearance of normal family life. Parents and children may try to hide the serious condition of the drinker. The strain on the rest of the family can become unbearable. The health and welfare of children may be put at risk. Neglect and physical abuse are common. Children may lose the attention of the drinking parent. Or they may become the victims of anger and beatings. They see the nondrinking parent being abused, and they are terrified. Children suffer embarrassment because of their drinking parent's behavior. They feel alone and helpless. They often have painful symptoms, such as headaches and nightmares.

The nondrinking partner and the children of an alcoholic may become victims of the alcoholic's anger.

IN THE WORKPLACE

Alcoholics often perform their work poorly, and this eventually affects the family. Alcoholics lose their ability to concentrate or to make decisions on the job. They lose the friendship, respect, and cooperation of other workers. Sometimes they provoke arguments, break equipment, and cause accidents on the job. They cost their employers money by staying home from work and using extra health benefits. They may be fired, and this causes hardship for their families. Then, too, their employers have the added expense of finding a new worker.

IN THE COMMUNITY

Researchers have found that alcohol plays a major part in the following:

▶ Accidental deaths
▶ Burns and deaths from fire
▶ Car crashes
▶ Drownings
▶ Falls
▶ Family court cases
▶ Homicides
▶ Hospitalizations
▶ Rapes
▶ Suicides

TEEN PREGNANCY

Over 1 million teens in the United States become pregnant each year. Most of these pregnancies are unplanned. Many of them occur because of alcohol or other drug use. Alcohol impairs judgment and causes the drinker to lose control of his or her behavior. People forget to practice safer sex. The result may be an unwanted pregnancy or a sexually transmitted disease, such as AIDS.

Babies born to mothers who drink alcohol during pregnancy may have many serious problems. Because the fetus (the developing baby) is so small, it will be affected by alcohol much more than the mother.

Birth defects may occur in babies born to mothers who drink. The babies may have fetal alcohol syndrome

(FAS). FAS babies may have vision or hearing problems. They may be missing some parts of their bodies. Their internal organs—including their brain—may be damaged. Some are so badly damaged that they die. The risk of FAS is so great that the federal government has enacted a law that requires alcoholic beverage containers to carry warnings about the dangers of drinking during pregnancy. Nonetheless, many women—teens or older—remain unaware of the risk they take by drinking when they are pregnant.

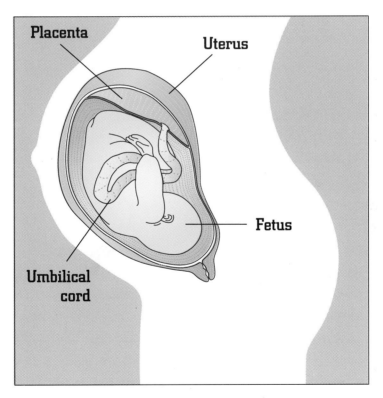

Alcohol is harmful to developing babies, especially during the first three months of pregnancy. Alcohol is absorbed through the placenta (the organ through which the fetus gets its nourishment) from the expectant mother's bloodstream.

DRINKING AND DRIVING

"My name is Sam. Two years ago, I was driving home from a special night out with my dad. It was about nine o'clock, and it was almost dark. We were talking about our night out when we saw a line of flares behind a car that was on the side of the road. Dad said, 'Let's see if we can help this guy.' He pulled over onto the shoulder and walked over to the man who was standing by the other car. I watched while the two of them talked for a minute. Then they crouched down and looked at a flat tire in the light from our headlights.

Suddenly, from behind, came the sound of a siren and the beams of headlights. Somebody was coming very fast. My dad and the man sort of stood up, shielding their eyes from the headlights, to see what was going on. Suddenly a speeding car swerved off the road and ran right into them! It hit them head on and drove right into the parked car! The noise was tremendous. The speeding car bounced around, hit the guardrail, and turned over.

I remember screaming 'Dad, Dad, watch out!,' but I was paralyzed by what I saw. A police car screeched to a halt. It had been following the speeding car. Two policemen jumped out and ran over to where Dad and the other man had been standing. I knew immediately that

Alcohol-related crashes cost society billions of dollars each year. But the loss of life is the greatest cost.

they had been crushed to death. They never had a chance.

We learned later that the speeding driver was very drunk. He walked away from the crash with only a few scratches, but my dad is gone forever. It's not fair. It's just not fair! **"**

Sam's tragedy could have happened to anyone. According to the National Highway Traffic Safety Administration (NHTSA), an estimated 16,589 people died in alcohol-related traffic crashes in 1994. That's an average of 1 death every 32 minutes.

Drinking and Driving: A Deadly Combination

The statistics listed here show how serious a problem drunk driving was just a few years ago. Are the roads any safer today? As of 1994:

▶ About 297,000 people suffered injuries in alcohol-related car crashes.

▶ About 2 of every 5 Americans will be involved in an alcohol-related car crash at some time in their lives.

▶ Male drivers involved in fatal crashes were nearly twice as likely to have been intoxicated (21 percent) as were females (11.1 percent).

▶ In the past decade, four times as many Americans died in drunk driving accidents as were killed in the Vietnam War.

▶ It is estimated that 1 of every 280 babies born today will die in a crash caused by a drunk driver.

▶ Traffic accidents are the major cause of death for children in the age group 0–14; almost a quarter of these deaths are alcohol-related.

▶ Children younger than 13 accounted for 19 percent of the U.S. population in 1994 and 6 percent of all motor vehicle deaths.

▶ Alcohol in combination with other drugs ranked second as a cause of death among children between the ages of 6 and 17.

Sources: NHTSA, *Facts*, 1994, 1995; Mothers Against Drunk Driving, *1995 Summary of Statistics: The Impaired Driving Problem; Annual Medical Examiner Data, 1994*, Drug Abuse Warning Network, U.S. Department of Health and Human Services

DRINKING AND THE LAW

It is illegal to drink in any state in the United States (except Louisiana) if you are under the age of 21. Yet in 1994, a survey conducted by the U.S. Department of Health and Human Services found that alcohol use among high school and college students was widespread. The survey discovered that:

▶ 56 percent of 8th graders have tried alcohol

▶ 71 percent of 10th graders have tried alcohol

▶ 80 percent of 12th graders have tried alcohol

▶ 88 percent of college students have tried alcohol

Many parents fail to tell their children clearly to avoid alcohol. When school-age children are allowed to drink alcohol at home, they are more likely to use alcohol and other drugs outside the home. They are also more likely to develop serious behavioral and health problems because of their use of alcohol and other drugs.

With this much underage drinking occurring, it is not surprising that more than 40 percent of deaths among 16- to 20-year-olds resulted from alcohol-related motor vehicle crashes.

According to a recent study, the average college student spends $446 a year on alcohol.

BLOOD ALCOHOL CONTENT

Alcohol in the bloodstream can be measured. The amount of alcohol in the bloodstream is called blood alcohol content (BAC). BAC is the percentage of alcohol contained in the blood after drinking. In other words, a BAC of 0.10 means that for every 1,000 drops of blood, there is 1 drop of alcohol.

As you read earlier, people react to alcohol in different ways. How they react depends on their weight, how often they drink, and how much they drink. But alcohol affects everyone's body and mind. In most states a BAC of 0.10 is the legal definition of intoxication (drunkenness). Because people were concerned about drunk driving, some states have dropped their BAC measurement of drunkenness to 0.08.

WHAT ABOUT TEEN DRUNK DRIVERS?

If a teen is stopped by the police for drunk driving, he or she will be treated like an adult. The police officer will ask the teen to take a breath test to measure his or her BAC. If the BAC is above the legal limit, the officer will arrest the teen. Teens who refuse to take the breath test will lose their licenses, even if they are not legally drunk. The teen who is arrested will have his or her car towed

More and more teens are arrested every year for drinking and driving.

away and will be taken to the police station and finger-printed. The police will call the teen's parents, who must pay the fines.

The teen will be charged with driving while intoxicated (DWI) or driving under the influence (DUI). DWI refers to alcohol alone; DUI refers to alcohol and other drugs. After a court trial, if found guilty of DWI or DUI, the teen can lose his or her driver's license for 90 days to a year. The teen will have to pay to get the license back and will have a police record. Some insurance companies may cancel the car insurance of a teenager who has been found guilty. The teen or the parents may have to pay for new, more expensive insurance. The teen may have to attend alcohol education classes.

ZERO TOLERANCE LAWS

Many states have special new laws for underage drinkers who drive. These are called zero tolerance laws. These laws state that for someone under the age of 21, any amount of alcohol in the blood is illegal. In some states the age drops to 18. More and more states are enacting these laws. Check your local laws; your state may have such a law.

The purpose of zero tolerance laws is to save lives. You have read about drunk driving. You have read the story of how Sam's father died. Let us hope that you never come closer than this to experiencing the senseless actions of a drunk driver.

How to Spot a
Drunk Driver

Here are some warning signs that can help you spot a driver who has been drinking. If you see any of these driving behaviors on the road, write down the license plate number and a description of the car. Stay away from that car. Call the police. <u>And never ride with a drunk driver!</u> A drunk driver might be:

▶ Driving across the centerline

▶ Driving with headlights off at night

▶ Driving 10 miles per hour or more below the speed limit

▶ Braking suddenly for no apparent reason

▶ Striking, or nearly striking, an object, such as the curb

▶ Driving on the wrong side of the road

▶ Weaving in and out of traffic or across the lane markers

▶ A driver who looks drunk, with eyes fixed and face close to the windshield, or even drinking in the car

Source: "Safe Party Guide," Mothers Against Drunk Driving.

WHY YOUNG PEOPLE DRINK

Germaine and Kim had been friends since third grade. They did everything together. But when the girls were in seventh grade, Kim made new friends. One day she invited Germaine to meet the new crowd after school. They would be down at the old boathouse by the river.

When Germaine and Kim arrived, Germaine was surprised to see that the other kids had beer with them. They were sitting on the floor of the boathouse, drinking and talking.

Germaine felt scared, and her stomach did flip-flops. "C'mon, Germaine," said Kim, offering her a beer. "Lighten up and have some fun."

Germaine simply froze. The scene was scary. She didn't know what to do. If she didn't go along with the crowd, they'd think she wasn't cool. She might lose her friendship with Kim, and people would make fun of her.

But something stopped her. When Kim urged her again to take a drink, Germaine took a deep breath and simply said that she didn't want to. Kim laughed at her and said that she was really out of it. And if she wasn't going to join in, she should just leave.

It took a lot of nerve and self-confidence for Germaine to walk out of the boathouse alone. It's very difficult to be laughed at by your best friend and embarrassed in front of other kids.

Not all underage kids drink. In fact, most don't. But to some, it may seem as if everybody's doing it. Peer pressure is one of the main reasons why young people drink. Peer pressure is part of preteen and teen behavior. You dress like your friends, and you listen to the same music. You want to fit in and be like everybody else. To be different is to risk being unpopular. Germaine must have felt very secure within herself. She was able to think through the situation on the spot and use her good sense. She knew the consequences of walking out, and she accepted them.

Not all young people are able to do that. Peer pressure can be very strong. Also, some young people feel shy in social situations. They don't want to stand out in the crowd. Fernando always looks for the guys who have a bottle when he goes to a party. "If I don't have a drink or two, I can't talk to anybody. Especially not a girl," he says. "And there's always a bottle somewhere. The guys ask their older brothers to buy it for them. Or they take it from their parents' supply."

Eileen says that she drinks to forget what's happening at home. Her parents have just split up, and there's a lot of unhappiness there. "I don't drink much. Just a wine cooler or two. They relax me, and I feel better."

These kids are responding to peer pressure and stress. They drink to feel better and forget their problems. They think that nothing bad will happen to

Wrong Information

Much of what you learn about alcohol from your friends may be inaccurate. Here are a few myths about alcohol:

Right? Alcohol makes you happy and gives you energy.

Wrong! Alcohol is a depressant. It may give you a lift at first, but it will soon slow you down and affect the way you think, talk, and move.

Right? Switching from one kind of drink to another—say, from liquor to beer—makes you more drunk than sticking to one kind.

Wrong! Alcohol is alcohol. Your BAC is what determines how drunk you are.

Right? A cup of black coffee and a cold shower will sober you up quickly.

Wrong! Nothing sobers you up but time.

Right? It's only beer. It's not strong enough to hurt you.

Wrong! Large amounts of any alcohol can damage your body and shorten your life.

Right? If you eat before drinking, you won't get drunk.

Wrong! Eating may slow down the effects of alcohol, but it won't stop the alcohol from entering your bloodstream.

Right? Drinking milk will coat your stomach and prevent you from becoming drunk.

Wrong! Drinking milk ahead of time will coat your stomach, and may also make you vomit when you drink alcohol. But it will not prevent you from becoming drunk.

Right? I can't do anything about a friend who is drinking too much.

Wrong! You can if you're a real friend! You can tell your friend how you feel about alcohol. You may not be able to change the person, but you will have shown your friend that you care about his or her safety.

Right? Drugs are a bigger problem than alcohol.

Wrong! Alcohol _is_ a drug. It kills more people than all other drugs combined.

Right? Alcohol makes you sexier.

Wrong! Alcohol reduces your inhibitions, so you may think that you are sexier. But since it also reduces your ability to think straight, you're on shaky ground. Drinking and sex don't go well together. The mixture can result in pregnancy, AIDS, car crashes, and more.

Right? Alcoholics are always drunk.

Wrong! Some people think that if they don't drink every day, they don't have a problem with alcohol. Alcoholics may not drink every day, or even every week. But when they do start drinking, they are unable to control how much they drink.

Right? My drinking affects only me.

Wrong! Don't think that it's your business alone. Your drinking can affect your family, your friends—everybody you know. And if you're old enough to drive, your drinking could endanger many more lives than your own.

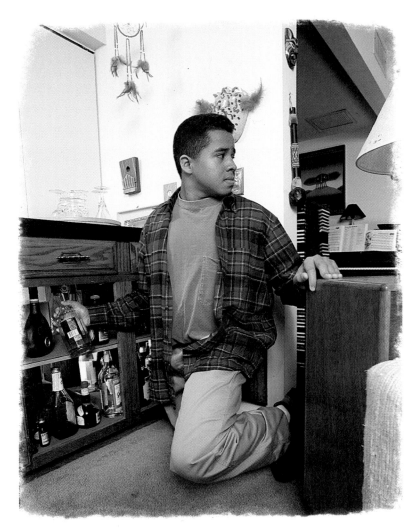

Although it is illegal for minors to buy alcohol, preteens and teens find other ways to obtain it, such as raiding their parents' liquor cabinets.

them. And since alcohol is so easy to obtain, they drink more. And the more they drink, the easier it is to abuse alcohol. Sometimes they become so confident that they begin to binge drink, and binge drinking is very dangerous.

AN ALCOHOLIC PARENT

Irene never invited her friends home after school. She hated to go home. To avoid going home, she joined lots of after-school activities. When she did go home, she'd often find her mother asleep in a chair. An empty glass was always nearby. The breakfast dishes would still be in the sink, and cigarette butts and ashes would be everywhere.

Irene knew that her mother had been drinking, but she didn't know what to do about it. Her mother's behavior frightened and embarrassed her. She felt alone and helpless.

An alcoholic is not just the dirty, ragged person you see sleeping in a doorway with an empty liquor bottle nearby. An alcoholic can dress nicely, go to work, live near you, and have a family and friends. An alcoholic can even be someone in your family. And if the alcoholic is one of your parents, you may be having a really bad time.

SIGNS OF ALCOHOLISM

Here are some signs that will help you tell if your parent may be an alcoholic:

▶ Alcoholics behave differently when drunk from when they are sober.

▶ Alcoholics lie about how much they have had to drink.

▶ Alcoholics drink more and more as time goes on.

▶ Alcoholics make excuses for needing a drink.

▶ Alcoholics hide bottles around the house.

▶ Alcoholics deny things they have said or done when they were drunk.

▶ Alcoholics' hands may shake.

▶ Alcoholics drink instead of eating.

▶ Alcoholics are not reliable and don't keep promises.

Even if you recognize only a few of these signs, you may have an alcoholic parent.

Children of alcoholics have a very hard time. The alcoholic parent has given up a healthy leadership role. The nondrinking parent may cover up for the drinking one. He or she makes excuses to everyone, even to the children. The children don't know where they stand with either parent. They are often left on their own. If the drinking grows worse, the children become frightened. They can't concentrate on schoolwork. They're afraid to ride in the car. They don't like holiday dinners, which usually end in drunkenness. They are afraid of violence and arguments. They may even experience

For children of alcoholics, holiday dinners are often times to dread because they end up in drunkenness.

physical abuse. They think that everything is upside-down and that something is wrong with them.

HOW FAMILY ROLES CHANGE

Little by little, normal family life breaks down. When the nondrinking parent makes excuses for the drinker, he or she often takes over that parent's role. It is natural to try to protect a loved one and keep a partner's weaknesses from the children. The drinker is dependent on alcohol, and the nondrinking parent becomes the enabler. The enabler thinks that he or she is helping but is actually making it possible for the drinker to drink more. When the drinker finds that there are no more responsibilities to take care of, drinking can take up more and more time. When the drinker forgets to pay the bills or loses a job, the situation has become very serious.

The children also may change. They may think that they are not being good enough and try hard to be better. They may feel guilty and think that they have caused the drinking. They try to do well in school. They do extra work around the house. Or, hurt and unhappy, they become troublemakers in order to be noticed. Other family members may think that the troublemaker is the cause of the drinking. Many children feel shame and anger at the same time. Some run away. Some become depressed. Some children simply become "lost." They retreat into a private world of their own making.

Some children of alcoholics become depressed by their parent's drinking problem and its negative effects on family life.

HOW TO SURVIVE IN THE FAMILY

If you find yourself in the family of an alcoholic, there are several ways to protect and take care of yourself. Work out ways with your family to keep the alcoholic out of the driver's seat of the car. Refuse to go in the car yourself if that parent drives. Watch out for fire—drinkers often smoke and are careless with their cigarettes. Find out what to do in a medical emergency. Be ready to call for help if the alcoholic has an accident in the house or goes into a coma. If you need to call, be sure to say that the person has been drinking.

If you or another family member is being physically abused, you must get help. This is sometimes difficult. It means telling on a parent. You may be taken from your home, at least for a while. But nobody deserves to be beaten and abused. Telling someone is the only way to stop the abuse.

You can't stop the alcoholic from drinking, but you can help yourself. You can love your parent but still hate his or her behavior. You should try to talk with your family about this—both with the alcoholic and with others. Expressing yourself may help to break the enabling circle of family behavior. Pick a quiet time, when the drinker is sober. Talking with a drunk person does not get the results you want.

Try to separate yourself from arguments and fights. Walk away, and remember it's the alcohol talking, not your parent. Ignore the insults. Stay out of arguments between your parents. Take up activities outside the home. Think up practical solutions to help run the house. If the place is a mess, maybe the family can hire someone to clean the house. If a brother or sister needs help with schoolwork, maybe you can help find a tutor. If you think it's risky to leave your alcoholic parent alone, you may have to stay home with him or her sometimes.

By making decisions and taking control of your life, you are helping yourself. And being a healthy, strong person yourself is the best way to help your alcoholic parent. Learn all you can about alcoholism. Talk to your friends who may have had similar problems. Stay involved with other people. It's harmful to remain alone.

Seek advice from someone you trust. You can't change your parent's behavior, but you can change your own. Many schools have counseling and drug abuse prevention programs. Talk to your teacher or guidance counselor. They can assist you in finding the help you need.

SUPPORT FOR THE ALCOHOLIC

Alcoholism exists, of course, because some people have not heard or paid attention to the facts about alcohol. And often alcoholics are not willing to admit that they have a serious problem. But since alcohol is readily available to everyone—even children—experts agree that education is the best way to prevent alcoholism.

Many schools have programs that educate students about alcohol. Driver education classes teach young people the dangers of drinking and driving. They also try to influence young people's attitudes about drinking. They teach values and decision-making skills.

Students Against Driving Drunk (SADD) is a nationwide organization in public schools. It was started by a teacher after two students died in accidents caused by drunk driving. You probably know its motto: "Friends don't let friends drive drunk." SADD uses a written "Contract for Life" between parents and teens. Teens agree to call their parents if they think that they are in a drunk driving situation. Parents agree to come to their children's aid.

Mothers Against Drunk Driving (MADD) is another nationwide organization. It was founded by a mother in California whose daughter was killed by a drunk driver. MADD members believe that education is very

Students Against Driving Drunk (SADD) and Mothers Against Drunk Driving (MADD) are two nationwide organizations that try to educate people about the dangers of drinking and driving.

important for preventing alcoholism. MADD members work hard for the passage of tough laws and stricter penalties for drunk drivers. They help victims of drunk driving when their cases go to court. And they follow up on parole hearings for convicted drunk drivers.

WHEN EDUCATION FAILS

Usually a family that is desperate enough finally seeks outside help. At first the family meets resistance from the alcoholic. With professional advice, the family learns that alcoholism is a continuing, or chronic, disease that cannot be cured. But the symptoms can be controlled—by not drinking.

Many alcoholics try hospitalization, therapy, and self-help groups. Treatment will not work, however, unless the alcoholic wants it to work. Sometimes it takes help to persuade the alcoholic to have treatment. There are many programs that provide help for families, for employees in the workplace, and for students in schools. Often, however, the alcoholic comes to his or her senses only after a terrible event. It may take an accident, a death, or the loss of a job to persuade the alcoholic to seek help.

Many alcoholics must then face detoxification, or "detox" as it is sometimes called. This is the first step in the withdrawal process, during which a person stops taking an addictive drug. Detox involves ridding the body of alcohol. It can be a difficult and uncomfortable physical and psychological experience. If people are in an advanced stage of alcoholism, they may have to detox in a hospital. They may sweat, shake, and have a rapid heartbeat. They may have hallucinations or delirium (feel and speak in a disordered way). They receive medication to help them through the process.

Finally, to avoid drinking again, alcoholics need therapy and support. There are many self-help groups, but the most famous of these is Alcoholics Anonymous (AA). AA has thousands of groups in many countries around the world. AA also has successful related groups. One is Al-Anon, which provides help for families and friends of alcoholics. Al-Anon, in turn, sponsors Alateen for teenage children of alcoholics.

Alcoholic preteens and teens can find help in many places. Help is available in hospitals, through family counseling, in live-in treatment programs or halfway houses, in schools, and in clinics.

WHAT YOU CAN DO

By reading this book, you have already learned a lot about alcohol and how it affects people. If you are concerned about underage drinking, here are a few things you can do:

▶ Continue to educate yourself and your friends about alcohol and alcoholism.

▶ Find the underage drinking statistics in this book or at your library, and make posters to hang at school.

▶ Write letters to the editor of your school paper or a local paper to discuss the problem of underage drinking.

▶ Encourage your friends to party sober. Help your parents and teachers to set up nonalcoholic graduation parties or other celebrations.

Protect yourself, your family, and your friends. Your knowledge and your actions count. Ask questions, state your opinions, and become involved. You can make a difference!

alcoholism: A dependence on alcohol.

binge drinking: Having more than five alcoholic beverages in one hour.

blackout: A temporary loss of vision, consciousness, or memory from too much alcohol.

blood alcohol content (BAC): Measurement of the percentage of alcohol in the blood.

chronic: Long-term or continuing, such as a chronic disease, as opposed to an acute, or short-lived, disease.

coma: A state of deep unconsciousness caused by injury, disease, or poison.

detoxification (detox): Removing a poison (alcohol or another drug) from the body.

enabler: A family member who, by protecting or making excuses for another family member who drinks, actually makes it possible for the alcoholic to drink more; also known as a codependent.

fetal alcohol syndrome (FAS): Birth defects that occur in babies born to women who drank during pregnancy.

gene: The basic unit of heredity; carries codes for individual characteristics.

hallucination: Something seen or heard that is not really there.

hangover: The unpleasant physical aftereffects of being drunk, including headache, fatigue, nausea, weakness, and thirst.

inhibition: Self-restraint.

malnourished: Lacking adequate food and nutrients.

placenta: The organ in the mother through which the developing baby gets its food.

tolerance: The ability of the body to resist the effects of a drug or a poison.

WHERE TO GO FOR HELP

Support Groups and Hot Lines

Alcoholics Anonymous (AA)
Look in your telephone
directory for local listings.

Al-Anon and Alateen
Look in your telephone
directory for local listings.

Al-Anon Family Groups
(Canada)
1-613-722-1830

Alcohol and Drug Treatment
Information Services
(Canada)
1-800-821-4357

Child Abuse Protection
Center (Canada)
1-613-771-6631
1-613-776-6060

Daytop Hot Line
1-800-232-9867

The Nineline
1-800-999-9999

Youth Crisis Hot Line
1-800-448-4663

International Organizations

United Nations International
Drug Control Program
United Nations
New York, NY 10017

National Organizations

Addiction Research Foundation
33 Russell Street
Toronto, ON M5S 2S1
1-416-595-6017

Alcohol and Drug Abuse
Association of North America
1101 15th Street, NW
Suite 204
Washington, DC 20005
1-202-737-4340

The Center for Substance
Abuse Treatment
1-800-328-9000

Mothers Against Drunk Driving
(MADD)
511 E. John Carpenter Freeway
Irving, TX 75062
1-214-744-6233

National Clearinghouse for
Alcohol and Drug Abuse
Information
1-800-729-6686

National Council on Alcoholism
and Drug Dependence
12 West 21st Street
New York, NY 10036
1-212-642-2944

Students Against Driving Drunk
(SADD)
P.O. Box 800
Marlboro, MA 01752
1-508-481-3568

Anderson, David. *College Alcohol Survey.* George Mason University, 1994.

Diamond, Arthur. *Alcoholism.* Overview Series. Lucent, 1992.

Harris, Jonathan. *This Drinking Nation.* Four Winds, 1994.

Holmes, Pamela. *Alcohol.* Drugs: The Complete Story Series. Raintree Steck-Vaughn, 1992.

Illegal Drugs and Alcohol. The Information Series on Current Topics. Information Plus, 1995.

Madara, Edward J., and Abigail Meese. *The Self-Help Sourcebook.* Saint Clare's–Riverside Medical Center, 1992.

McMillan, Daniel. *Winning the Battle Against Drugs: Rehabilitation Programs.* Franklin Watts, 1991.

Monroe, Judy. *Alcohol.* The Drug Library. Enslow, 1994.

Mothers Against Drunk Driving. *1995 Summary of Statistics: The Impaired Driving Problem.* August 1995.

Ryerson, Eric. *When Your Parent Drinks Too Much.* Facts On File, 1985.

Shuker, Nancy. *Everything You Need to Know About an Alcoholic Parent.* The Need to Know Library. Rosen, 1990.

Vogler, Roger, and Wayne Bartz. *Teenagers and Alcohol: When Saying No Isn't Enough.* Charles Press, 1992.

Wijnberg, Ellen. *Alcohol.* Teen Hot Line Series. Raintree Steck-Vaughn, 1994.

INDEX